PLAY LIKE A GIRL
SOCCER

BY
EMILIE DUFRESNE

KidHaven PUBLISHING

Published in 2020 by
KidHaven Publishing, an Imprint of Greenhaven Publishing, LLC
353 3rd Avenue
Suite 255
New York, NY 10010

Edited by: Madeline Tyler
Designed by: Danielle Jones

Cataloging-in-Publication Data

Names: Dufresne, Emilie.
Title: Soccer / Emilie Dufresne.
Description: New York : KidHaven Publishing, 2020. | Series: Play like a girl | Includes glossary and index.
Identifiers: ISBN 9781534530973 (pbk.) | ISBN 9781534530065 (library bound) | ISBN 9781534531291 (6 pack) | ISBN 9781534530911 (ebook)
Subjects: LCSH: Soccer--Juvenile literature.
Classification: LCC GV943.25 D847 2020 | DDC 796.334--dc23

Printed in the United States of America

CPSIA compliance information: Batch #BS19KL: For further information contact Greenhaven Publishing LLC, New York, New York at 1-844-317-7404.

Please visit our website, www.greenhavenpublishing.com.
For a free color catalog of all our high-quality books, call toll free 1-844-317-7404 or fax 1-844-317-7405.

IMAGE CREDITS

Cover - TungCheung, AlexRoz, wxin, inthevisual, khun nay zaw, zartae292. 3 - wxin. 4 - sirtravelalot, irin-k . 5 - muzsy, Ververidis Vasilis, OSTILL is Franck Camhi. 6 - muzsy , Philippa Bass, Leicestershire & Rutland County FA, Venus Angel. 7 - A_Lesik, Rawpixel.com, alexkatkov. 10 - Roka Pics, Oleksandr Osipov. 11 - Pete Saloutos, Tungphoto. 12 - Nikelser. 13 - Nikelser, Webspark. 14 - leolintang, Oleksandr Osipov. 15 - Veniamin Kraskov, J. NATAYO, wavebreakmedia, Martel, Levent Konuk. 16 - urbanbuzz, xjrshimada. 17 - Ververidis Vasilis, P Maxwell Photography, SumanBhaumik. 18-19 - tovovan. 20 - supot phanna, Influential Photography, Onur Kocamaz. 21 - Dziurek, Fotokostic. 22 - Monkey Business Images, Christian Bertrand. 23 - Influential Photography. 24 - EL Loko [GFDL (http://www.gnu.org/copyleft/fdl.html) or CC BY 4.0 (https://creativecommons.org/licenses/by/4.0)], from Wikimedia Commons, Pierre-Yves Beaudouin [CC BY-SA 4.0 (https://creativecommons.org/licenses/by-sa/4.0)], via Wikimedia Commons. 25 - Jamie Smed from Cincinnati, Ohio [CC BY 2.0 (https://creativecommons.org/licenses/by/2.0)], via Wikimedia Commons. 26 - Mascha Tace, irin-k, PAS Images. 27 - STILLFX. 28 - Dana Roesiger, Heinrich-Böll-Stiftung [CC BY-SA 2.0 (https://creativecommons.org/licenses/by-sa/2.0)], via Wikimedia Commons, New Africa. 29 - Dazzlefleck, Ampatent [CC BY-SA 3.0 (https://creativecommons.org/licenses/by-sa/3.0)], from Wikimedia Commons, monticello, Daboost. 30 - Ljupco Smokovski, wavebreakmedia. Illustrations by Danielle Jones.
Images are courtesy of Shutterstock.com. With thanks to Getty Images, Thinkstock Photo and iStockphoto.

CONTENTS

Words that look like this are soccer lingo. Learn more about them on page 8.

Words that look like THIS are explained in the glossary on page 31.

THE BASICS

TEAM HUDDLE

So, you want to play soccer? This book will teach you all about what to say, what to wear, and how to play. From learning the lingo to earning a place in the Hall of Fame, this book will give you the know-how!

GRAB YOUR FRIENDS AND A BALL – IT'S TIME TO PLAY!

Soccer, called football in many countries, is a game played by two teams. Each team can have up to 11 players on the field at a time. Players use their feet to kick and dribble the ball around the field to try to score goals by putting the ball in the opposing team's goal.

Soccer is a very challenging game that requires a high level of fitness. Soccer players have to be able to perform under pressure, work together as a team, and practice lots of passing and dribbling skills to be able to win a game.

Soccer is a contact sport. However, there are rules restricting how much contact players can make. The referee has to decide when too much force has been used or too much contact has been made. If this happens, the referee calls a foul and gives a free kick to the side the foul was committed against.

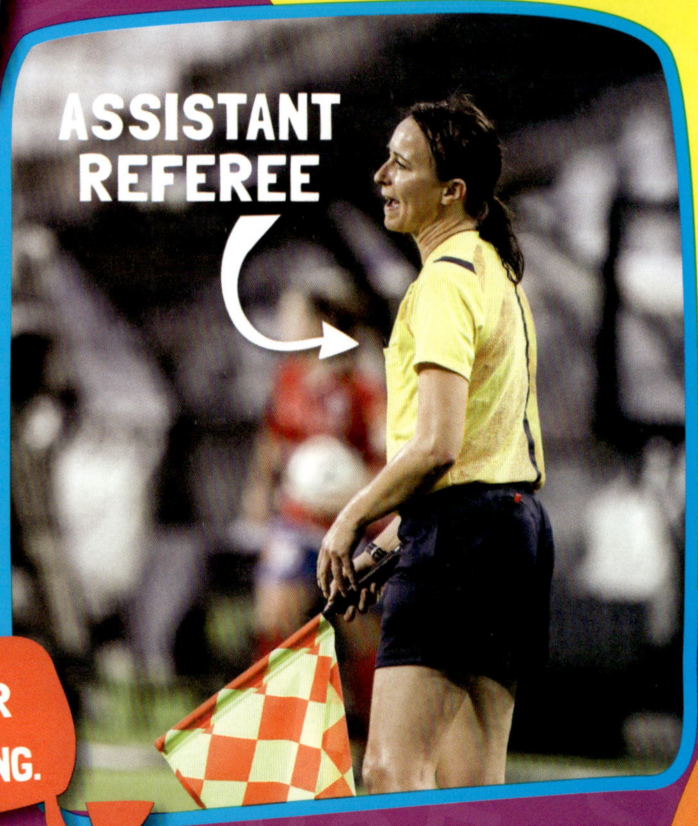

TAKE A LOOK AT PAGE 21 FOR MORE INFORMATION ON FOULING.

THE TYPES

FUTSAL

Futsal is a type of soccer that is played on an indoor court that is smaller than an outdoor field. Each game is five-a-side and the games are shorter than the normal game, having only two 20-minute halves.

BLIND SOCCER

Like futsal, blind soccer is also five-a-side with two 20-minute halves. It is a variation of soccer and futsal. Blind soccer is for people who are blind, but there are also variations for people with different levels of **VISUAL IMPAIRMENTS**. The ball contains metal **BALL BEARINGS** that make noises as the ball moves. This lets the players know where the ball is.

YOU CAN FIND OUT MORE ABOUT SPORTS FOR PEOPLE WITH VISUAL IMPAIRMENTS ON THIS WEBSITE: IBSASPORT.ORG.

BEACH SOCCER

This is a type of soccer that is played on sand instead of grass. This makes the style of play very different. Players need to be able to **IMPROVISE** and work with the sand. Players are allowed to score from anywhere on the field. This speeds up the game and means that in an average match there is a goal every four minutes.

ZORB SOCCER

As well as wearing a normal uniform, zorb soccer players also wear a large inflatable ball over their bodies! This lets players bounce into one another and makes it a lot harder to score a goal.

THE LINGO

The lingo, the slang, the vocab. Whatever you call it, learning the words behind specific sports can be a very daunting task! Here are some of the terms and weirder words that will help you talk the soccer talk in no time.

DEFENSIVE

A way you can organize your team on the field that focuses on defending.

KNOCK-OUT GAMES

A type of match in a competition where only one team can progress to the next level of the competition. One team must win this type of match, so the teams can't draw.

QUALIFYING GAMES

The series of matches that a team must go through in order to compete in certain competitions such as the World Cup and the Olympics.

OFFENSIVE

A way you can organize your team on the field that focuses on scoring.

THROW-IN

A throw given to a team when one of their opponents was the last person to touch the ball before it went off the side of the field.

MANAGERS

The person or people who run a soccer team. They do important tasks such as motivating players and selecting which players should play when and where.

COACHES

These can be instructors, trainers, and teachers that are there to help the players improve their abilities.

DRAW

When both teams score the same amount of goals in a game.

FIVE-A-SIDE

A type of soccer where each team can have five players on the field at any one time.

PENALTY KICK

A free shot that is taken from the penalty spot. It is a one-on-one battle between a player and a goalkeeper. No other players are allowed inside the penalty box.

PENALTY SHOOTOUT

When both teams take turns taking penalty kicks after a draw in order to determine the winner of a knock-out game.

TACTICS

Actions or strategies that can be put in place to improve a team's chances of scoring and to stop their opponents from scoring.

THE PLAYERS

There can be 11 players per team on the field at any time. These players can be put into four main categories: goalkeepers, defensive players, midfielders, and forwards. Players can be arranged on the field in different ways depending on how they want to play.

MIDFIELDERS

As the name suggests, midfielders play in the middle of the field between the defenders and the attackers. Midfielders are very VERSATILE players and can play both a defensive and offensive role. It is their job to try to get the ball from their end of the field up to the opponents' half.

ATTACKERS

Also known as the strikers, these are the forwards that try to score goals. They play near the opposing team's goal and have to try to skillfully get around the opposing team's defenders to create scoring opportunities.

GOALKEEPER

There is only one goalkeeper on the field per team. It is their job to try to stop the ball from going into their goal. They usually spend most of the match in their own penalty area. They are allowed to use their hands inside their own penalty area and are allowed to wear goalkeeper gloves to help them grip the ball and protect their hands.

DEFENDERS

It is the defenders' job to defend the area in front of their team's goal. These players should tackle opposing players that have the ball, block any shots, and **INTERCEPT** passes between opposing players. If they manage to get control of the ball, the defenders then pass to the midfielders to get the ball farther up the field.

FORMATIONS

A formation is a type of pattern the players stand in when on the field. You can use different formations to play different types of games.

Soccer formations are written in the form of a sequence of numbers. For example, a 4-4-2 formation is where there are four defenders, four midfielders, and two attackers. Since the goalkeeper is always positioned near the goal, they aren't included in these names.

On page 13, the players in red are positioned in a 5-3-2 formation. This is a more defensive formation with lots of midfielders and defenders to stop the opposing team from scoring goals.

The players in blue are positioned in a 4-3-3 formation. This is a more offensive formation as there are three attackers ready to try to create scoring opportunities.

There are lots of different variations of formations that a soccer team can use. Players must be able to think quickly and change the plan or formation to best suit whatever situation they face.

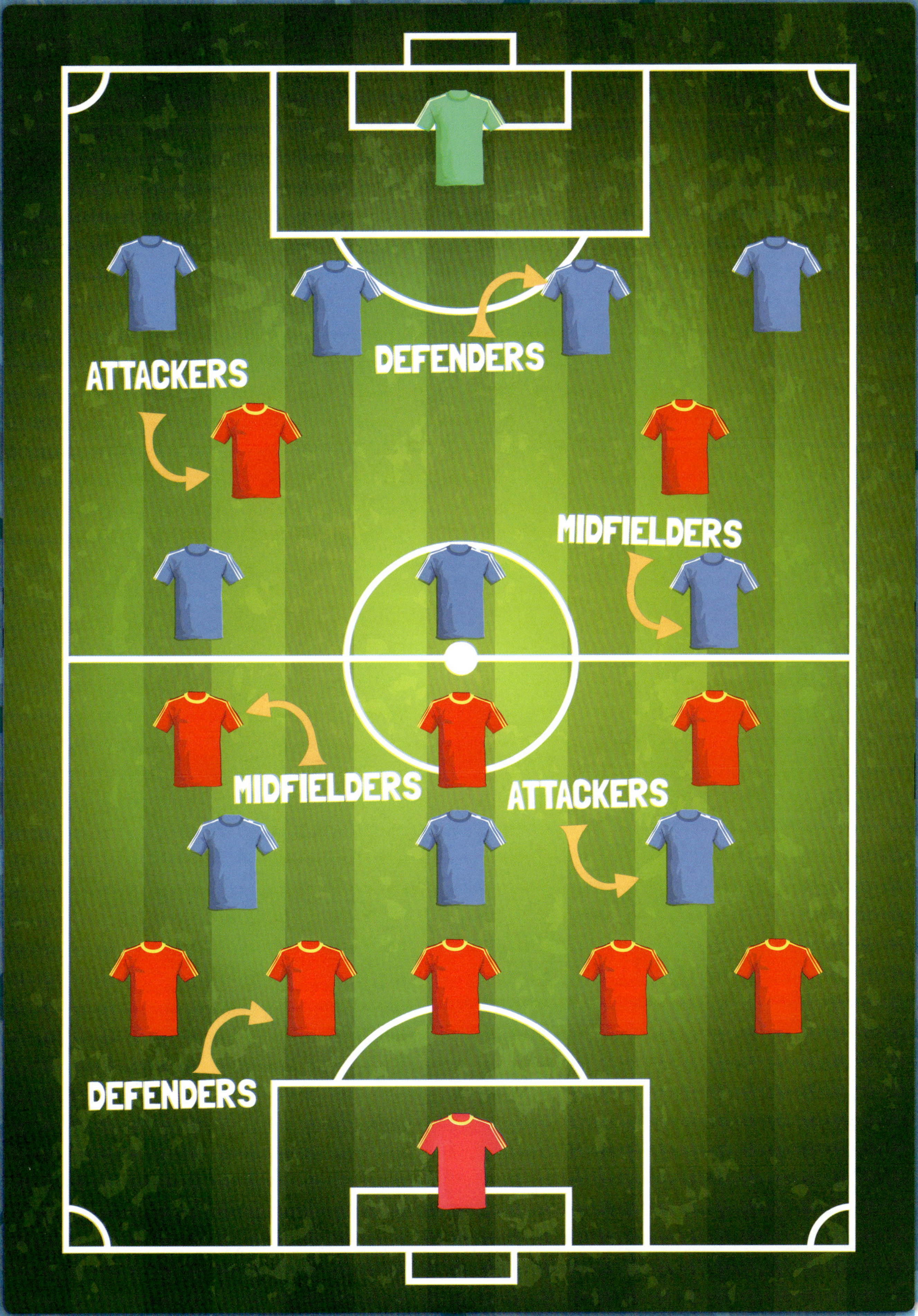
DEFENDERS
ATTACKERS
MIDFIELDERS
MIDFIELDERS
ATTACKERS
DEFENDERS

THE UNIFORM

Soccer is a fast-paced sport that needs both STAMINA and strength. It is important to make sure you are wearing the correct clothing and protective gear to allow you to perform your best and not get hurt while doing so.

A soccer player's outfit usually consists of a short-sleeved, lightweight shirt that is made of BREATHABLE fabric. On the bottom, players usually wear baggy shorts that are just shorter than knee length. This gives players freedom of movement to be able to run, jump, and make daring shots and passes.

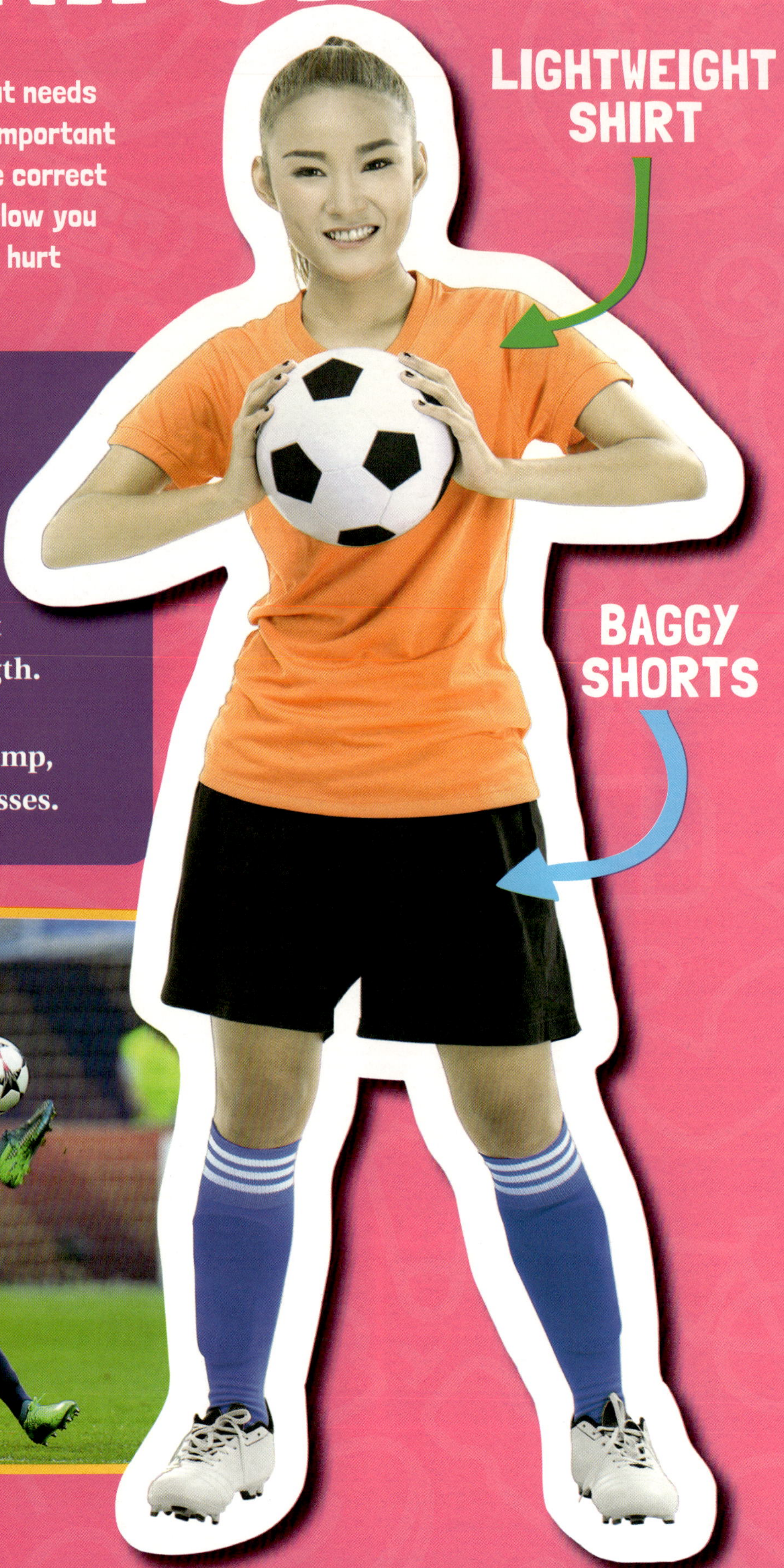

If playing on grass, **PROFESSIONAL** soccer players use cleats with studs on the bottom of them. These studs help players to grip the ground and stop them from slipping or sliding on the grass.

CLEATS

There is also protective gear that is important to wear. This includes shin pads. These are worn inside players' socks and protect their legs from other players' cleats.

Beach soccer is played barefoot.

SHIN PADS

SOCCER GLOVES

THE EQUIPMENT

THE BALL

A standard soccer ball must be between 27 inches and 28 inches (68 and 70 cm) in circumference and weigh between 14.5 ounces and 15.9 ounces (410 and 450 g).

STANDARDIZED OBJECTS MAKE SURE THAT THE GAME IS FAIR BY MAKING SURE EVERY GAME IS PLAYED WITH THE SAME TYPE OF EQUIPMENT EVERY TIME.

THE GOAL

A professional, full-sized goal has a distance of 24 feet (7.3 m) between the two goal posts. The height of the goal is 8 feet (2.4 m). Junior matches often use smaller goals. They use goals that are 7 feet (2.1 m) high with posts that are 21 feet (6.4 m) apart.

CORNER POSTS

Corner posts and flags are positioned at each corner of the field. If the ball goes out of play, these help the referees tell whether the ball has passed the touchline, resulting in a throw-in, or the goal line, resulting in a goal or corner kick.

OFFSIDE FLAG

REFEREE EQUIPMENT

It is important that the referee and assistant referees have the right equipment. Some essential pieces of equipment they need are whistles, red and yellow cards, and flags. These help the referee get the attention of the players and clearly show their instructions.

RED AND YELLOW CARDS

WHISTLE

THE FIELD

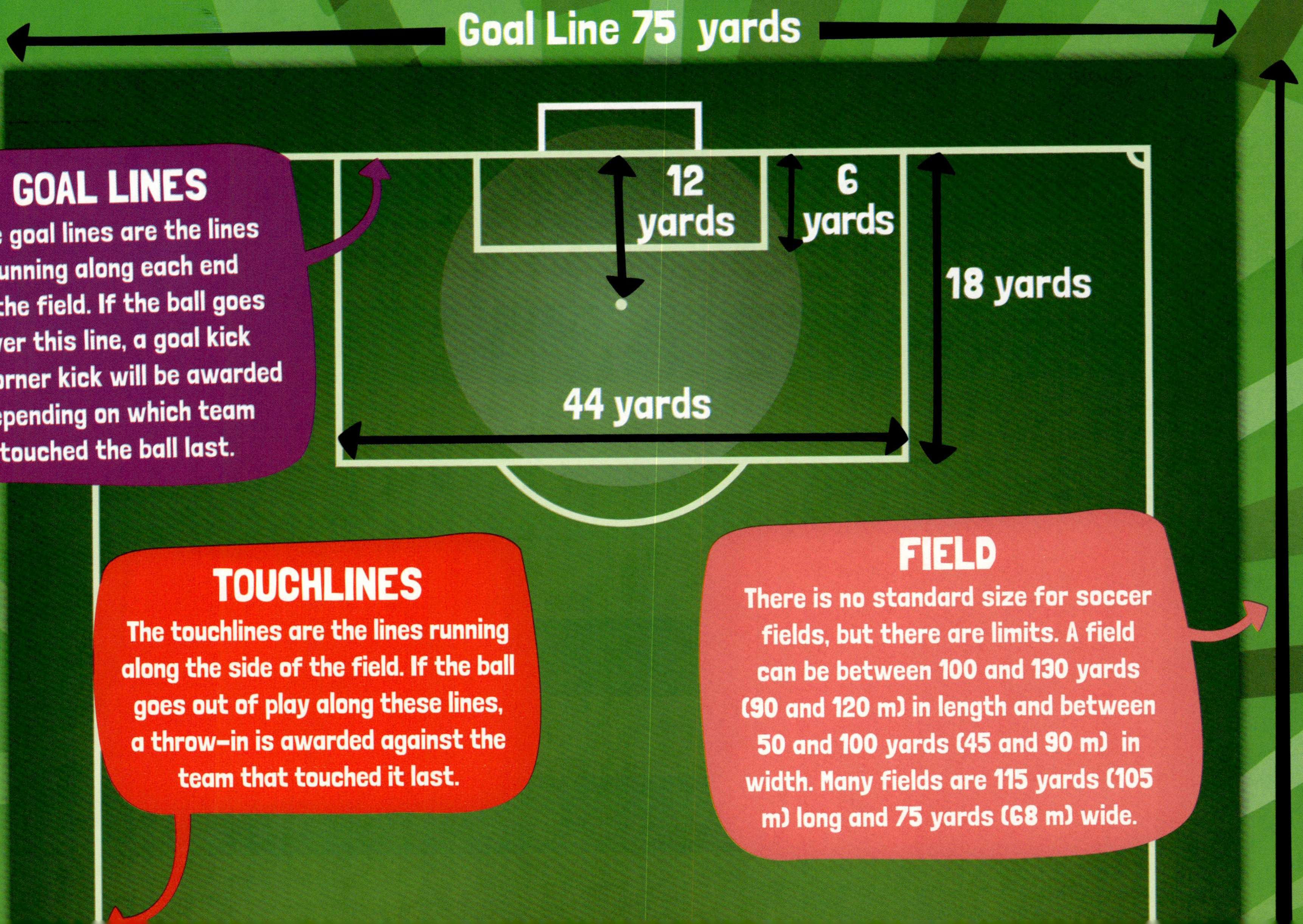

GOAL LINES

The goal lines are the lines running along each end of the field. If the ball goes over this line, a goal kick or corner kick will be awarded depending on which team touched the ball last.

TOUCHLINES

The touchlines are the lines running along the side of the field. If the ball goes out of play along these lines, a throw-in is awarded against the team that touched it last.

FIELD

There is no standard size for soccer fields, but there are limits. A field can be between 100 and 130 yards (90 and 120 m) in length and between 50 and 100 yards (45 and 90 m) in width. Many fields are 115 yards (105 m) long and 75 yards (68 m) wide.

Touchline 115 yards

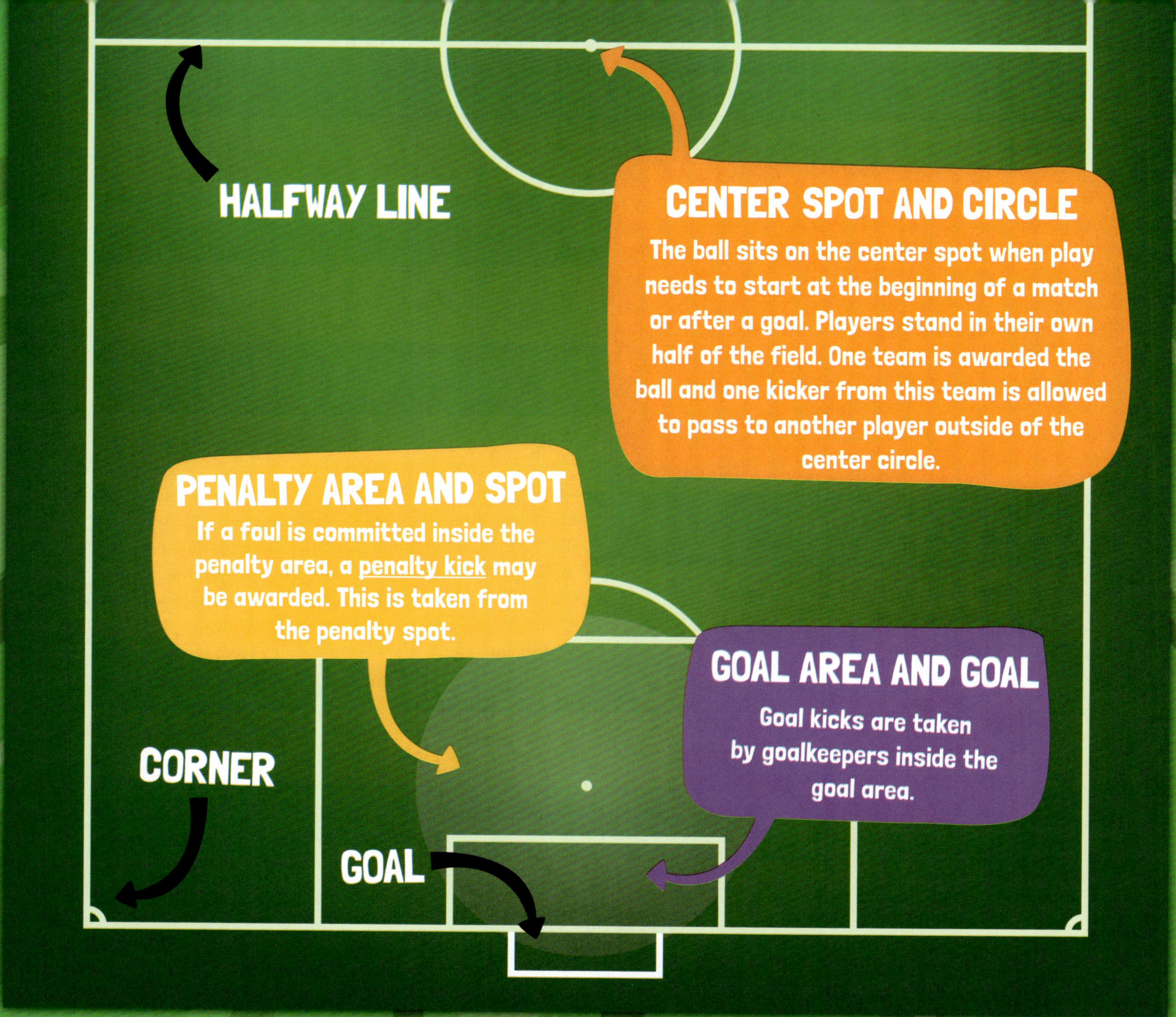

CENTER SPOT AND CIRCLE

The ball sits on the center spot when play needs to start at the beginning of a match or after a goal. Players stand in their own half of the field. One team is awarded the ball and one kicker from this team is allowed to pass to another player outside of the center circle.

PENALTY AREA AND SPOT

If a foul is committed inside the penalty area, a penalty kick may be awarded. This is taken from the penalty spot.

GOAL AREA AND GOAL

Goal kicks are taken by goalkeepers inside the goal area.

THE RULES

TIMING

A soccer match is split into two 45-minute halves. Between the two halves is a halftime interval of up to 15 minutes when players can **REHYDRATE** and discuss tactics with the managers and coaches. If time is lost during either half due to substitutions or injury, a referee can choose to add extra minutes onto either half of the match to make up for the time lost.

EXTRA TIME AND PENALTIES

In knock-out games, there can't be a draw, as a winner must be decided. If there is a draw, then there is extra time added. This is made up of two 15-minute halves. At the end of this time, if the score is still equal, then a penalty shootout takes place.

FOULING

A foul occurs when a player does something against the rules while playing. The most common fouls are caused by one player kicking, tripping, pushing, or charging another player. Often, fouls are called when a player tries to make a tackle but contacts the player before contacting the ball.

IF A DEFENDER COMMITS A FOUL IN THEIR OWN PENALTY AREA, THEN A PENALTY IS AWARDED TO THE OPPOSING TEAM.

FREE KICKS AND PENALTIES

After a foul has taken place, a free kick may be given to the team the foul was committed against. They are allowed to take this kick without any opponents trying to tackle or defend against them.

PLAYER TAKING A FREE KICK

THE EVENTS

RECREATIONAL AND REGIONAL TEAMS

If you have a school team, or a team that plays RECREATIONALLY, and you want to start competing, there are lots of ways you can get involved. Ask a teacher, parent, or sports coach how to join a local league.

AMATEUR SOCCER TEAM

FC BARCELONA, 2018

THE BIG LEAGUES

As soccer players get better and better, they can start playing at higher levels. Soccer players can play for a club that represents a certain region or area. These teams often have their own levels of competition, with the best teams playing in the best leagues. There are also lots of competitions where national teams can play countries from the same CONTINENT as them, such as the Africa Women's Cup of Nations, the European Women's Championship, and the Women's Asian Cup.

THE OLYMPICS

The Olympics is a very **PRESTIGIOUS** competition where countries from all over the world can come and compete in lots of different games, one of which is soccer.

Women's soccer was added to the Summer Olympics in 1996.

BRAZIL VS. SWEDEN, 2016 OLYMPICS

THE WORLD CUP

Perhaps the most famous international soccer tournament is the World Cup. The Women's World Cup was first held in 1991 in China. National soccer teams from across the world compete in qualifying games to take one of 23 places in the tournament. The 24th place is taken by the nation that hosts the tournament.

ENGLAND VS. WALES, WORLD CUP QUALIFIER, 2018

THE ONES TO WATCH

There are some very talented female soccer players on the rise. Let's find out some more about them.

FRAN KIRBY

FACT FILE:

Date of Birth:
June 29, 1993

Country of Birth:
United Kingdom

Height:
5'2" (1.57 m)

Position:
Forward

Kirby's first senior international appearance was at the 2015 FIFA Women's World Cup in Canada. Since then she has just kept improving her skills. In 2018, her hard work was recognized, and she was named the Professional Footballers' Association's (PFA) Young Player of the Year.

ADA HEGERBERG

FACT FILE:

Date of Birth:
July 10, 1995

Country of Birth:
Norway

Height:
5'10" (1.77 m)

Position:
Forward/Striker

At a young age, Hegerberg already has many titles to her name. In 2016, she won UEFA's Best Women's Player in Europe and Norwegian Sportsperson of the year. Then in 2017, she was awarded the BBC's Women's Footballer of the Year. In 2018, she won the first ever Women's Ballon d'Or.

PLAY LIKE A GIRL

SYDNEY LEROUX

FACT FILE:

Date of Birth:
May 7, 1990

Country of Birth:
Canada

Height:
5'7" (1.7 m)

Position:
Forward

One of the best strikers in soccer, Leroux is a formidable forward. Originally playing for Canada, she now plays for the U.S. national team. It was with this team that, at the age of just 22, Leroux won an Olympic Gold medal.

HOPE SOLO

FACT FILE:

Date of Birth:
July 30, 1981

Country of Birth:
USA

Height:
5'9" (1.75 m)

Position:
Goalkeeper

Arguably the best female goalkeeper on the scene, Solo is definitely a goalkeeper to watch out for. Internationally, she has helped the U.S. national team win two Olympic gold medals and a World Cup. She also has numerous individual awards for her excellent goalkeeping skills.

THE HALL

There is a great history of female soccer players. Let's take a look at some of the best of the best.

Marta Vieira da Silva is one of the best female soccer players of all time. This brilliant Brazilian has won FIFA World Player of the Year an astonishing five times. She also holds the record for the most goals scored at World Cup tournaments. She is now one of the most **DECORATED** female soccer players of all time.

Homare Sawa was a Japanese soccer player who had a very impressive international career. She is one of only two players to have ever competed in six World Cup tournaments, one of which she captained to victory in 2011. For this she was awarded FIFA World Player of the Year in 2011.

OF FAME

Mia Hamm was an iconic American soccer player who has multiple achievements to her name. One of these is being part of the national team that went on to win the first ever women's Olympic gold. Her achievements didn't stop there. In 2013, Hamm became the first woman to be inducted into the World Football Hall of Fame.

Nadine Angerer was a great German goalkeeper. She has been awarded three Olympic Bronze medals and has won two FIFA World Cup tournaments. Individually she was awarded FIFA Women's World Cup Best Goalkeeper in 2007 and FIFA World Player of the Year in 2013.

THE FACTS AND STATS

THE YOUNGEST FEMALE TO PLAY IN A WORLD CUP MATCH WAS BIRGIT PRINZ, WHO REPRESENTED GERMANY IN THE WOMEN'S WORLD CUP FINAL IN 1995 AT JUST 17 YEARS OLD!

AS OF EARLY 2019, THE COUNTRY THAT HAS WON THE MOST FIFA WOMEN'S WORLD CUP TOURNAMENTS IS THE USA, WINNING THREE IN TOTAL.

THE HIGHEST GAME OF SOCCER EVER PLAYED WAS ON MOUNT KILIMANJARO IN 2017 AT 18,747 FEET (5,714 M) ABOVE SEA LEVEL! THIS WAS COMPLETED BY 32 FEMALE PLAYERS WHO CLIMBED THE MOUNTAIN FOR A CHARITY THAT PROMOTES GENDER EQUALITY IN SPORTS, CALLED EQUAL PLAYING FIELD.

TO FIND OUT MORE, GO TO EQUALPLAYINGFIELD.COM.

IN 2018, THE JAMAICAN WOMEN'S FOOTBALL TEAM (ALSO KNOWN AS THE REGGAE GIRLZ) BECAME THE FIRST CARIBBEAN TEAM TO QUALIFY FOR THE FIFA WOMEN'S WORLD CUP.

CARLI LLOYD HOLDS THE RECORD FOR FASTEST GOAL SCORED IN A FIFA WOMEN'S WORLD CUP FINAL. IT ONLY TOOK HER THREE MINUTES FOR HER FIRST GOAL AND SHE WENT ON TO SCORE THE FASTEST HAT TRICK AS WELL, SCORING THREE GOALS IN AN AMAZING 16 MINUTES!

SOCCER IS ONE OF THE MOST POPULAR WOMEN'S SPORTS IN THE WORLD, WITH 176 TEAMS COMPETING INTERNATIONALLY.

YOUR TEAM

If soccer sounds like the sport for you, why not try to get a team together. Ask all your friends if they want to give it a go. If you have a gym or an outdoor field at your school or where you live, why not try it?

If you enjoy playing soccer, why not keep practicing? You never know, you might be in the Hall of Fame one day!

GLOSSARY

amateur	someone who does something for fun rather than professionally
ball bearings	small metal balls
breathable	something that lets air pass through it
continent	a very large area of land that is often made up of many countries, such as Africa and Europe
decorated	in a profession, this is when you have been given awards, medals, or trophies for your work
FIFA	Fédération Internationale de Football Association; an organization that oversees international competitions such as the World Cup
gender equality	when both men and women have the same rights and opportunities as each other
improvise	to think on your feet and work with what you have at any given time
intercept	to stop something from moving in a certain direction and change its direction of movement
prestigious	having an important and highly regarded status
professional	doing something you are good at as work
recreationally	to do something for fun rather than professionally
rehydrate	to drink plenty of liquids after exerting yourself
stamina	ability to maintain physical or mental effort
UEFA	The Union of European Football Associations; an organization that oversees soccer in Europe
versatile	able to be adapted in order to fit many different functions or activities
visual impairments	limited or reduced vision

INDEX

PLAY LIKE A GIRL

FIELD HOCKEY

BY

EMILIE DUFRESNE

KidHaven
PUBLISHING

Published in 2020 by
KidHaven Publishing, an Imprint of Greenhaven Publishing, LLC
353 3rd Avenue
Suite 255
New York, NY 10010

Edited by: Robin Twiddy
Designed by: Danielle Jones

Cataloging-in-Publication Data

Names: Dufresne, Emilie.
Title: Field hockey / Emilie Dufresne.
Description: New York : KidHaven Publishing, 2020. | Series: Play like a girl | Includes glossary and index.
Identifiers: ISBN 9781534531000 (pbk.) | ISBN 9781534530096 (library bound) | ISBN 9781534531321 (6 pack) | ISBN 9781534530942 (ebook)
Subjects: LCSH: Field hockey--Juvenile literature.
Classification: LCC GV1017.H7 D847 2020 | DDC 796.355--dc23

Printed in the United States of America

CPSIA compliance information: Batch #BS19KL: For further information contact Greenhaven Publishing LLC, New York, New York at 1-844-317-7404.

Please visit our website, www.greenhavenpublishing.com.
For a free color catalog of all our high-quality books, call toll free 1-844-317-7404 or fax 1-844-317-7405.

IMAGE CREDITS

Cover - DeanHarty, Vereshchagin Dmitry, 3DMAVR, India Picture, Supertrooper, Ben Jeayes. 3 - Rob Byron, V.S.Anandhakrishna. 4 - SpeedKingz, Ben Jeayes, Alexander Kalina. 5 - mooinblack, EcoPrint. 6 - EcoPrint, Lorraine Swanson. 7 - Dhodi Syailendra. 8&9 - peterboxy, Zovteva, By Stacy Barnetta. 10 - ostill, Aspen Photo. 11 - EFECREATA.COM, Rob Wilson, Supertrooper. 12 - Corepics VOF. 13 - Ice_AisberG. 14 - Jacob Lund. 15 - Halfpoint, Rob Wilson. 16 - DeanHarty, Raul Topan, J. NATAYO. 17 - Zovteva, Ben Jeayes. 18 - Ice_AisberG. 19 - Boris Ryaposov, dotshock. 20 - Corepics VOF. 21 - Corepics VOF, mooinblack. 22 - Corepics VOF, almonfoto, mooinblack. 23 - Corepics VOF, Mai Groves. 24 -Munihd [CC BY-SA 4.0 (https://creativecommons.org/licenses/by-sa/4.0)], from Wikimedia Commons, fourthandfifteen [CC BY 2.0 (https://creativecommons.org/licenses/by/2.0)], via Wikimedia Commons. 25 - fourthandfifteen [CC BY 2.0 (https://creativecommons.org/licenses/by/2.0)], via Wikimedia Commons, fourthandfifteen [CC BY 2.0 (https://creativecommons.org/licenses/by/2.0)], via Wikimedia Commons. 26 - Chones, Africa Studio. 27 - STILLFX. 28 - Skumer, Corepics VOF, mooinblack. 29 - MH STOCK, Sam Aronov, fourthandfifteen [CC BY 2.0 (https://creativecommons.org/licenses/by/2.0)], via Wikimedia Commons. 30 - v Rawpixel.com, Aspen Photo, nipastock. Illustrations by Danielle Jones. Images are courtesy of Shutterstock.com. With thanks to Getty Images, Thinkstock Photo and iStockphoto.